Chappell Roan

Icon of our times

her life. her music. her style.

Carolyn McHugh

sona BOOKS

First published in the UK 2025 by Sona Books an imprint of Danann Media Publishing Ltd.

CAT NO: SON0654

Photography courtesy of

Getty images:

Jim Bennett
Vivien Killilea
Mary Mathis for The Washington Post
Stewart Cook/CBS
Rebecca Sapp / Stringer
Maya Dehlin Spach/FilmMagic
Nina Westervelt/Billboard
Natasha Moustache
Christopher Polk/Billboard
Erika Goldring
John Shearer
Gilbert Flores/Variety
Lisa Dragani
Kevin Mazur
Jim Dyson
Sonja Flemming/CBS
John Shearer
Axelle/Bauer-Griffin/FilmMagic
Rick Kern
Axelle/Bauer-Griffin/FilmMagic
Gilbert Flores/Billboard
Dania Maxwell / Los Angeles Ti
Marleen Moise
Josh Brasted/FilmMagic
Jason Kempin
Katja Ogrin/Redferns

Alamy images:

Sipa US/Alamy Live News
Andy Von Pip/ZUMA Press Wire
Amy Harris/Invision/AP
Timothy Swope
Patti McConville
CraSH/imageSPACE /MediaPunch
Geisler-Fotopress GmbH
Amy Harris/Invision/AP
Kristoffer Tripplaar
Sergey Skleznev
xmpi04x Credit: Imago
Mpi04/Media Punch
United Archives GmbH
Kathy Hutchins
Ted Hsu
Alex Garland
Vinyls
Sandra Dahdah/ZUMA Press
Alive Coverage/Sipa USA

Other images, Wiki Commons

Cover concept Audrey Alexander
Book design concept Darren Grice at Ctrl-d
Proof reader Juliette O'Neal

Printed in UAE.

ISBN: 978-1-917259-22-4

Contents

Chappell Roan:

Introduction

rammy award-winning Chappell Roan has brought queer culture to the forefront of pop since exploding onto the mainstream music scene in summer 2024 with her catchy songs, headline-grabbing performances and drag-inspired looks.

From small town dreams to worldwide fame, the meteoric rise of Midwest pop princess Chappell is a story of creativity, resilience, and artistic evolution.

Her journey to stardom has actually been 10 years in the making – starting when she was just 16 and spotted on YouTube singing covers and a few original songs back in 2014. After a false start, and interruption from a pandemic, the world turned its attention to Chappell in 2020 with her breakout single *Pink Pony Club*.

Since then she has built a body of work that cheerleads for queerness - celebrating self-expression, embracing one's true identity, and revelling in life's highs and lows.

Cut to 2024 and her extraordinary debut album, *The Rise and Fall Of A Midwest Princess* has stormed the charts, her single *Good Luck, Babe!* was the hit of the summer, and not only has she headlined a world tour, but she has played to record-breaking festival crowds.

Chappell Roan lights up the 2025 GRAMMYs stage with a fiery performance of *Pink Pony Club*

Her 2025 win of Best New Artist at the Grammy Awards cemented her breakout success. Now everyone is talking about the genre-defying young American singer-songwriter with a lengthy line of crowd-pleasing, '80s inspired, anthemic dance pop tracks that radiate and celebrate queer culture.

Yet while Chappell exudes creative energy around her drag queen aesthetic and confident performances, beneath all the colour and pizzazz is a refreshing and unapologetic blend of vulnerability and authenticity which has seen her emerge as the voice of her tribe.

A self-proclaimed 'DIY Pop Princess', Chappell has cultivated a devoted fanbase, all inspired by her raw, honest approach to pop music.

Superlatives swirl around her like glitter, with *Rolling Stone* christening her as 'The Future of Pop', UK music magazine *NME* calling her 'the most exciting new pop star in the world right now', and *Music Business Worldwide* dubbing her the biggest breakthrough artist of 2024.

This book takes a deep dive into her creative process, tells the stories behind her most iconic songs, and looks at the fashion evolution that has made her a refreshingly fearless and larger-than-life icon.

Dive into Chappell Roan's story to experience the powerful journey of an artist who dares to be different and do things her way...

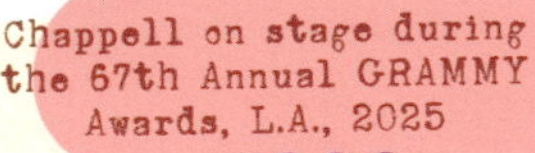

Chappell on stage during the 67th Annual GRAMMY Awards, L.A., 2025

The birth of Chappell Roan

Chapter 1

happell now plays to crowds larger than the population of the town she grew up in. Willard is a small town of around just 6,000 people in Springfield, Missouri, USA.

Accounts of her childhood and early family life vary, and she is vague about it herself. While some reports have her growing up in a trailer park, other versions of her story place her as firmly middle class. She told BBC Radio 1 that she lived briefly in a trailer park when she was 'really little – then we had a house'.

Her home community was very conservative and religious and not a place where Chappell, known by her birth name of Kayleigh Rose Amstutz back in those days, felt able to express any kind of showmanship. As she got older she began to feel increasingly out of place.

She attended church three times a week with her family, parents Kara and Dwight and three younger siblings, and would even spend some summers at Christian camps. Expanding on her upbringing during an interview with Variety magazine in 2023, she said 'I just wanted to feel like a good person, but I had this part of me that wanted to escape so bad'.

The cover of *Kayleigh Rose* EP, 2014

She found some escape in pop music, which she loved, with Britney Spears being an early favourite, along with The Spice Girls, Lady Gaga and Kate Bush. She began taking piano and singing lessons but didn't get along very well with formal coaching. She did have one early small success when she won her school's talent show in what was her first public performance, aged 13, singing *The Christmas Song*. Less successfully, she auditioned for the TV show 'America's Got Talent' but didn't make it through to the televised rounds.

However, true ambition had taken hold as she hit her early teens so she began to write songs of her own and upload covers to YouTube. In 2014 she released an 11-minute EP called *Kayleigh Rose*, including four songs, *Die Young*, *Crave You*, *Tell Me Again* and *I Don't Love You*.

One of her early compositions, the ballad *Die Young*, which she wrote at a summer camp, can still be viewed on YouTube. It was a striking enough composition and performance to further her YouTube following, and even earned her a shout out from Australian singer-songwriter Troye Sivan who told his Twitter followers that he had 'this 16-year-old girl on repeat...You have to listen to this guys, show some love'.

Despite that early validation, Chappell nowadays describes that track as 'the corniest song on earth'.

The YouTube performance, which attracted 15,000 YouTube views after the Sivan boost, shows a 16-year-old Kayleigh Rose with long, curly dark blonde hair singing straight to the camera while accompanying herself on keyboard.

Follow

i've had 16 year old girl on repeat for 2 months. you HAVE to listen to this, guys - go send some love. youtube.com/watch?v=G1mGN6...

11:06 PM · 11/4/14 From Earth

Speaking to Tom Power, host of the CBC arts and entertainment podcast Q, she said that her original reason for uploading music onto YouTube was to help her break into acting. But when people began saying that she had a good voice, she started posting music, imagining it could be a way into acting. She knew that Madonna had done something similar as a way into becoming a dancer, so that's not a bad path to retread.

Chappell chat

'I **really thought** I was going to be an **actress**. I thought **music** would be a **gateway into acting** and it ended up being my **actual job**.'

Speaking to Tom Power on CBC arts and entertainment podcast Q in 2024.

Eventually, her long imagined escape came – courtesy of a record deal with Atlantic Records.

'I was just a YouTube girl, they found me on YouTube', she told Power. 'I'd written some songs at summer camp and posted them and got discovered'.

However, record companies tend to offer lots of developmental deals to young artists in the way of placing small bets and hoping that some will pay off. Several major labels asked her to showcase for them, so she went to New York to play a few gigs and had several offers before choosing Atlantic. She signed to them in 2015 for five years in a deal she now describes as 'horrible' as a minor at age 17 and, as she puts it ...'she didn't know anything about the business'.

Her parents were equally unaware of the ins and outs of the music industry – her father was a nurse who had retired from the Navy, while her mother was a veterinarian.

It makes her laugh to remember that the news of her record deal was announced over the loudspeaker at her school ...but in the same sentence as the information that the day's lunch option was pizza. 'Everyone said, "she's lying"' Chappell told Q.

But it was all true and she was on top of the world, dropping out of high school a year early to have the time to develop this new career. Although, with hindsight, Chappell has described having mixed feelings about missing her graduation and final year, telling *Vanity Fair* in a 2023 interview, 'I don't miss high school... But I miss my youth. I mourn being a kid because my career took that away from me pretty immediately when I signed.'

However she did sign the deal with Atlantic, and she signed it after carrying out one more big, important change – a name change.

As well as growing up feeling out of place and isolated in her community, she also remembers always having felt unconnected to her own name, Kayleigh.

So her transformation to pop star began with the decision to adopt an alter ego – and in doing, so she took the opportunity to pay homage to her maternal grandfather.

'I have never felt super connected to my real name Kayleigh. My grandfather's name was Dennis K. Chappell, so I took Chappell in his honour,' she told *Cherwell*, the student magazine of Oxford University. 'Before he passed away in 2016 due to brain cancer, I told him that I was going to be Chappell for him. Roan came from his favourite song, which was called *The Strawberry Roan*, an old Western song about a pinkish red horse. It's a very sentimental name. I do still wish my name was not Kayleigh in real life, though.'

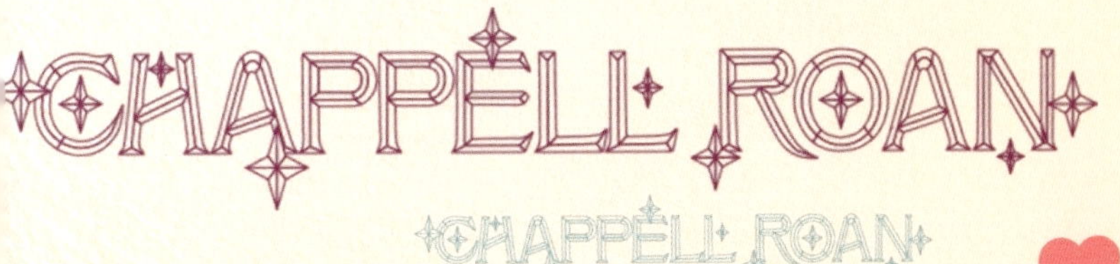

Strawberry Roan

The Strawberry Roan is a classic American cowboy song. The lyrics come from a poem, first published in 1915 by a Californian cowboy called Curley Fletcher, which describes the challenges and adventures of a cowboy trying to ride a wild horse.

It later became a hugely popular cowboy song, considered one of the greats of its genre, with its catchy melody and vivid story leaving a lasting impact on Western and cowboy culture.

Sung by various artists over the years, the most famous recording of The Strawberry Roan is the 1959 version by country and western singer Marty Robbins, included on his album Gunfighter Ballads and Trail Songs.

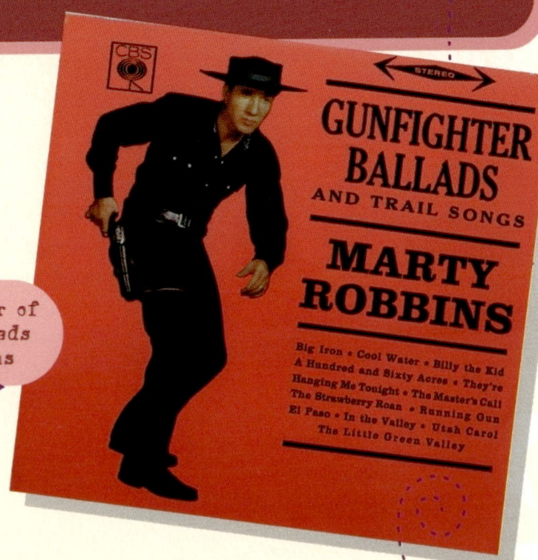

Vinyl record cover of *Gunfighter Ballads* by Marty Robbins

Alter ego in place, Chappell Roan left Kayleigh Rose behind her and headed east and west to New York and LA, recording and performing to kick off her career...

Just landed

Birthday: 19 February 1998
Height: 1.57m
Early influences: Kate Bush, Keesha, Bratz Dolls
First concert: Hannah Montana, supported by the Jonas Brothers

Chappell chat

'At the very beginning, I was doing a lot of dark synth pop. It was ballady, witchy, and melodramatic. I listened to Lana, Lorde, and Ellie Goulding my entire high school.'

Speaking to Pop Crave in 2023 about her musical inspirations.

Breaking into music Version 1.0

Chapter 2

Breaking into music: Version 1.0

Immediately after signing her record deal, Chappell continued living at home with her family, but frequently travelled coast to coast all over America as she promoted her music.

In 2017 she released her first music as Chappell Roan, the single *Good Hurt* and the EP *School Nights*, both of which showcased her distinctive voice and lyrical prowess. Hopes were high all round that these music releases would introduce her to a wider audience and signal the start of a promising career.

The process of creating and promoting her debut EP *School Nights* was a formative and massive learning experience, and also highlighted her adaptability and willingness to experiment with different musical styles.

But reviewing that folk-leaning work now, Chappell speaks about the music being 'boring' and 'uninspired', lacking the sparkle and pizzazz she now sprinkles liberally into her compositions.

An EP photoshoot conducted by Catie Laffoon, 2017

School Nights EP (2017)

Track list

- Die Young
- Meantime
- Bad For You
- Good Hurt
- Sugar High

Certainly those songs are slower and more downcast than the pop bangers which make up most of her sets these days. The album is moody and dark, and it's all a bit sad girl bedroom singer-songwriter music. Her cursive singing style – using long vowels, note sliding and lack of diction - doesn't show off the full strength of her vocals. Yet, evoking comparisons with powerhouse vocalists including Lorde and Adele, she was still a strong and compelling singer-songwriter and a good notch above most of her contemporaries.

So much so that she picked up some major gigs as a supporting artist, first for Australian indie musician Vance Joy (for the American leg of his 2017 *Lay It On Me tour*) and then from January – March 2018 for English singer-songwriter Declan McKenna on the American leg of the tour for his debut album *What Do You Think About the Car?*

This opportunity to perform, and just as crucially to see close up how the headliners performed, was another formative experience for Chappell as she realised she didn't like singing sad, slow songs and wanted to change to a more crowd-rousing, upbeat sound.

'I hated performing my old EP on tour,' she told US entertainment website *Vulture* in 2023. '[Declan] would jump off the speakers, and throw balloons in the crowd, and have so much fun every night. I was like, I want to do that. I don't want to do what I'm doing. This is too serious. How do I have fun on stage? How do I make this a party?'

Re-energised and beginning to settle on her style, Chappell made the decision to relocate permanently to LA in 2018 when she was aged 20.

And this is when she really found herself.

Chappell chat

'...the pendulum has swung so far the other way. I don't think I would have been as outgoing and obnoxious if I had been from the coasts.'

Live on stage at The Showbox, Seattle, 2017

'It was definitely a transition to move to LA, California. I just had a really hard time feeling understood and I was so confused about my emotions and about what art meant to me,' Chappell told Sian Eleri on the Radio 1 Interview Podcast in May 2024.

'It was a difficult time. It took a while to really grasp who I am as an artist, but I guess that's just for everyone that's young. They just have a hard time grasping who they are. It took a while to make friends, because I didn't go to college so I didn't have friends my age for a while.'

'Then through going to drag shows and through music I started to make more and more friends, especially in the queer community.'

As well as finding her feet socially, Chappell found freedom in LA which allowed her to question and explore her personal identity. She went into therapy and spent time connecting with her 'inner child', which she found helpful and inspiring.

Chappell chat

I think L.A. and New York give me this freedom to be whatever I want and wear whatever I want.

She also met the man who would become her main collaborator, producer and songwriting partner, Dan Nigro. Dan had worked with artists including Kylie Minogue, Finneas, Lewis Capaldi and Caroline Polachek since his own move to LA, from New York.

Together they ventured into the competitive music industry. And things would never be quite the same again...

Dan Nigro and Chappell Roan attend Spotlight Saturdays at the GRAMMY Museum L.A. Live, 2024

It's gonna cause a scene

It's gonna cause a scene - Pink Pony Club

Chapter 3

2020 marked a pivotal moment in Chappell Roan's career with the creation of her breakout single, *Pink Pony Club.*

The cover art for *Pink Pony Club*, bathed in pink and radiating euphoria

The inspiration for the song came from a deeply personal place as it reflected her own journey of self-discovery and acceptance. Having relocated to Los Angeles from her small hometown in Missouri, Chappell found herself immersed in a vibrant and diverse community that celebrated individuality and freedom of expression.

Feeling that she could at last be herself, without fear or judgement, Chappell was inspired by this unfamiliar environment. With her creativity ignited by her new life and her professional partnership with producer Dan Nigro, she and Dan wrote Pink Pony Club to capture the essence of the joy and liberation Chappell found while embracing her true self and a place where she belonged.

Chappell often describes the song as a love letter to the queer community. It tells the story of a small-town girl dreaming of dancing as a stripper in a West Hollywood nightclub, against the wishes of her family. Although it was written before she adopted her drag persona and came out as gay, those feelings were all bubbling under and the ideas were popping up in her music.

The idea for the song crystallised after Chappell had visited her first gay club - the famous Abbey bar in West Hollywood. Her lyrics symbolise her own aspirations and the courage it took to pursue them. Sung over an upbeat tempo and with an infectious chorus, the synth-pop song was a big change from Chappell's earlier work but marked the start of something big for her ... even though she would wait a few more years for her mainstream and commercial success, which came in 2023 after the release of its parent album *The Rise and Fall of a Midwest Princess*.

Back in 2019 Atlantic didn't want to release the track, believing that it was too different from the music she was making when they had signed her. There's no denying it was quite a shift from her earlier sound, and that's one of the reasons the relationship between Chappell and Atlantic began to break down.

However, Chappell fought hard against the label's decision for a year before persuading Atlantic to relent, and the song was eventually released on April 3, 2020.

billboard

RollingStone

Chappell's faith in her song was fully vindicated when *Pink Pony Club* was met with huge acclaim from fans and critics. Publications including *Rolling Stone* and *Billboard* highlighted the song as a standout track of 2020. With prescience, *Rolling Stone* said 'Chappell Roan's *Pink Pony Club* is an anthem for self-discovery and acceptance, marking her as a powerful new voice in pop music.'

The song was also successful on streaming platforms, rapidly climbing the charts and earning spots on several high-profile playlists.

Glowing neon allure in the *Pink Pony Club* official music video

YouTube

The accompanying music video is also worthy of a watch on YouTube where it currently has over 22 million views. Featuring Chappell performing before her drag look, the video is nonetheless filled with drag queens and other club-goers, showcasing the people who embody the diversity and creativity of the community that inspired the song and giving due notice of what was to come from Chappell in the future.

Directed by Griffin Stoddard, the vibrant video created a fantastical and inclusive atmosphere to complement the song's themes of freedom and self-expression. Chappell collaborated closely with the director and choreographer to ensure that every element reflected her vision. The story opens with Chappell's face lighting up as she steps into the dimly lit club, a world of neon lights, glitter, and exuberant dancing. As the video progresses, different scenes highlight the joy and acceptance Chappell finds in her new surroundings.
The climactic dance sequence, set against a backdrop of twinkling lights and confetti, symbolises the ultimate celebration of self-love and community.

But the year 2020 is also in the history books for a different reason - the Covid-19 pandemic and consequent worldwide lockdowns. This was financially damaging and terrible for the entertainment industry as a whole, with all live performances cancelled. But for an emerging artist like Chappell it was particularly cruel as she couldn't build on her early promise. 'I was so devastated,' she said. 'It made me second-guess myself.'

Then speaking to Pop Crave she said 'It was actually very sad, because .... It was a very dark time when it came out. No one could party, and it was West Hollywood's anthem! It's for going out and queerness, and it was just so sad that I couldn't perform it.'

Cinematic moments from the dancefloor in the Pink Pony Club official music video

Then things got worse. Despite the overall success of *Pink Pony Club*, and her other follow up releases for Atlantic, *Love Me Anyway* and *California*, she was dropped by the record label, which cited 'underperformance' as the reason.

It obviously wasn't the end of her story, as in the years following *Pink Pony Club,* Chappell Roan has continued to evolve as an artist. Yet despite the changes in her look and trajectory, the song remains a defining moment in her journey. It encapsulated a time of transformation and self-discovery, setting the stage for the iconic artist she would become.

As can be seen in her performance of the song on 2 November 2024 when she made her debut on the US institution *Saturday Night Live* show, where she is in full drag persona, it still works perfectly four years later.

Chappell chat

'Pink Pony Club came from me wanting to be a Gogo dancer in LA but, truthfully, I'm not confident enough to do that, so I wrote a song about it.'

Speaking to Cherwell magazine in 2022.

The Rise and Fall of a Midwest Pricess album cover

Following Chappell's rise to fame after the release of *The Rise and Fall of a Midwest Princess* where it is included as track 11, the song has charted in the UK's Top 20 and the US Top 30. It was also featured during Chappell's appearance on the video concert series 'NPR Tiny Desk' and used as the closing song/encore at major music festivals, including Chappell's record-breaking show at Lollapalooza in Chicago in August 2024.

The song has now been streamed over 180 million times, and rising, on Spotify.

'It feels so good to prove them wrong because they weren't just a little wrong, they were really, really, really wrong,' Chappell told *Rolling Stone* magazine in autumn 2024, speaking of her old team at Atlantic. 'To know that my gut instinct was right is the best feeling in the world. Purposeful revenge does not feel good, but revenge by accident feels awesome.'

Breaking into music

Chapter 4

ropped by Atlantic – and forced to move back home to Willard during the pandemic lockdowns – Chappell felt her dreams were in shatters.

Losing a record deal, with all the promise around it, and having to come back home is challenging to say the least. On top of that, her four year relationship with a boyfriend had ended around the same time. She was also diagnosed with a bipolar condition – although at least that provided some answers around certain aspects of her behaviour, 'My parents just thought I was being a brat so I had such a difficult time', Chappell told *Variety* afterwards.

Understandably she came close to giving up on music altogether, still smarting from her experience facing the complexities of the music industry, including the pressures of commercial success and the demands of record labels. Balancing artistic integrity with industry expectations was a recurring challenge, leading to her eventual decision to pursue an independent career.

Scenic view of West Los Angeles

'Like any artist, there's a level of self-doubt in a situation like that,' Chappell's manager Nick Bobetsky reflected when speaking to *Music Business Worldwide* in 2024. 'But there are two very different paths when an artist gets dropped: one is that they're deflated and destroyed because they put so much weight on the fact that they were with a major label; the other is that they're inspired by knowing that they now truly hold the reins, there is no one telling them what they should or shouldn't do.'

And in the end Chappell took the path of optimism, deciding to give music one more try. She rolled up her sleeves and worked as a barista in a drive-through coffee shop to help her make enough money to get back to Los Angeles.

Once back out west in LA in 2021, she gave herself a year to make it. She has said in various interviews that her only alternative plan involved going back to college to train either as an aesthetician or a geneticist.

But in the meantime she was fired up and ready for a second stab at making it big. Money was still an issue, and as she pieced her life and career back together, she worked all sorts of jobs including time as a nanny, a production assistant, and even in a doughnut shop.

But all her spare time was devoted to making music and working on the songs which would eventually come to be her pop-perfect debut album, *The Rise And Fall Of A Midwest Princess*.

What got her through was the confidence she had in herself and her work.

'I knew I had Pink Pony Club under my belt and I knew people loved that song and I loved it. So I knew if I kind of followed that direction it would be great,' she told the Radio 1 Podcast Interview in May 2024. 'I really just needed money to fund the project, it was getting too big and difficult to manage myself. I was doing a lot of inner-child therapy at the time and I realised that the thing I needed to do was honour the part of myself that was this glittery, dress up, a lot of makeup part of myself that I adored when I was eight or nine years old. I started honouring her and my whole life changed, the aesthetic was born and it was all very natural.'

Chappell chat

'I've never put pressure on myself to be this clean, chic, well-put-together pop girl. I've always wanted to look a little tacky, a little bold, maybe a little controversial. I think that's what honours my inner child. I think she deserves the utmost respect of expression.'

In fact, in an interview with *Glamour* magazine in May 2023, Chappell explained why she now believes that being dropped was one of the best things that happened to her, explaining that ...' it really tested what I was made of. I was very, very close to quitting. I thought that I would go to school and just not do music anymore. I ran out of money, I was living with my parents during the pandemic. I was working the drive-through. Like a lot of us were. A lot of us lost our jobs. And so I think that emotional journey wasn't very different from the average person's journey of, like, defeat. And a little bit of a rock bottom. But that's why, now, it's so amazing, because I realised how far I've come. And there's all this stuff I really appreciate and try not to take for granted.'

In November 2021, Chappell had picked up the pieces and reconnected with producer/songwriter Dan Nigro. While Chappell had been away, Dan had had a huge hit producing Olivia Rodrigo's chart-topping, debut album *Sour*. So it was an exciting time for the pair of them to reunite. Dan had been convinced of Chappell's talent since they had first worked together on *Pink Pony Club*.

'Pink Pony Club is one of my favourite little combos of songwriting with anybody I've ever had in my life', he told Fast Company in a 2024 interview .'I was just so enthralled [with] what she was creating and what she had to say.'

As Dan's reputation grew from his work with Olivia Rodrigo, Chappell began to enjoy some success herself as slowly, slowly, the buzz around Pink Pony Club was reaching cult proportions. It was turning out to be a huge sleeper hit, pushed by Tik Tok clips, rather than promotion by the music industry 'proper'.

TikTok

Chappell credits Dan with persuading her to begin working independently. 'Dan was just looking at me and goes, "You are going to run your career into the f****** ground if you don't start doing s**t on your own",' she told *Rolling Stone.* So that is what she did, and now describes it as 'the best thing that could've happened to my career'.

Chappell dazzling in satin, sparkle and shimmer in the *Naked in Manhattan* official music video

In March 2022 Chappell released her debut single, *Naked In Manhattan* as a completely independent artist. She shot her own music video, with friends on the streets of New York City, wearing thrift store/charity shop clothing.

The song hinted that she was beginning to question her own sexuality. Although she had a boyfriend when she wrote it, the song captures her feelings for a girlfriend, with lyrics like, "Boys suck, and girls I've never tried it," expressing her desire to explore a same-sex relationship.

It was as an independent artist that Chappell began finding a new audience as her music began leaning into queer culture.

She also won vast numbers of fans when she got the chance to open a couple of huge gigs in 2022, including for Olivia Rodrigo during her 'Sour' tour and for artist Fletcher during her 'Girl of My Dreams' tour.

Chappell continued to release independent singles, including *My Kink Is Karma* in May 2022 and *Casual* in October that same year.

'[Being independent] lit a fire under my ass', Chappell said in an interview with Capital Buzz. '[...] I did what I always wanted to do... which is, like, release music whenever I wanted to, dress however I wanted to... I felt like, '"Damn, I was meant to do this, because it's working without a label".'

However, she did go on to sign a deal in January 2023 with Amusement Records, the imprint her close collaborator Dan Nigro had founded at Island Records. She had succeeded independently and had nothing to prove there, while Nigro's label offered her the chance to develop her professional and creative relationship with Dan.

The creation of Amusement Records was not just a business decision but a commitment to Chappell's career.

Roan posing for a portrait in her dressing room at the House of Blues, Chicago, 2023

Nigro's belief in Chappell's talent and potential has been pivotal and his establishment of Amusement Records allowed him and Chappell to release music without the constraints of larger labels.

The next step for Chappell came when she set about changing her image, developing the look she's known for today, but in a scrappy way. She began developing the DIY-Princess look with which she became famous - red curls, makeup and elaborate burlesque-style costume - though her fully developed drag look was still to come. At last she felt comfortable in her performance skin.

Making magic together

Dan Nigro
Chappell's chief collaborator

Grammy award-winning American record producer, songwriter and musician Dan Nigro has been a key member of Chappell's team since her earliest days in Los Angeles. He is responsible for helping her to shape and amplify her special sound.

He had his own successful career as a performer in the early 2000s with his emo band As Tall as Lions, who toured extensively and cracked the Top 100 with their third album, *You Can't Take It With You*.

You Can't Take It With You album cover

But New Yorker Dan tired of touring and moved to LA in search of making it big as a songwriter when the band split in 2010. He linked up with childhood friend and now fellow producer, Justin Raisen and got his start composing promotional jingles for the likes of McDonalds.

Before long he and Justin began getting more rewarding and high profile work with Sky Ferreira, Carly Rae Jepsen and Kylie Minogue.

'Dan just has a knack for songwriting," Ariel Rechtshaid, a three-time Grammy winner who also worked with Dan during his early days in LA, told *The New York Times*. 'He's always been interested in what makes a great song, but also in songs that don't necessarily sound like anything else that's working in pop music.'

But it was when he was in his mid-30s and reached out to a young Olivia Rodrigo after coming across her on social media that Dan's career became super-charged. He suggested that they collaborate, and now – two smash-hit albums Sour and Guts, and 16 Grammy nods later – the rest is history.

He and Rodrigo were named 2024 Songwriters of the Year by ASCAP, Olivia Rodrigo is now among the biggest pop starts on the planet and Dan is a world famous, in-demand producer. Now, he simply continues to blow up the charts with his collaborations with Chappell Roan.

Dan Nigro and Olivia Rodrigo at the Variety Hitmakers event, Los Angeles, 2024

He's very happy to be a behind-the-scenes impresario these days. Recalling his time as a performer during an interview with *Music Business Worldwide*, he said, 'Once we started touring and were on the road all the time, I realised how much I hated not having a routine and I found myself quite disconnected from reality at some points. You're living in this weird alternate bubble, where you're moving around, going from show to show, you're in a new city, you show up at a venue, you're performing and then getting back in the van and doing it all over again.

'The allure wore off quite quickly for me and I realized I like creating music more than I like performing it. You can show up to a venue and have 500 fans that love you, but still be losing money on the show. That's really tough to deal with, being completely broke the entire time.'

Now married with a child, and his own imprint, Amusement Records, Dan can pick and choose his work – and he chooses Chappell.

He recognised her talent incredibly early in her career, when she was first in LA under the pre-pandemic Atlantic deal. As had happened with Olivia, Dan just had a conviction that Chappell was something special.

'It was the third day. We started to write her song *California* and I just knew. I don't know what it was, but I was like, "This person is really special." I became obsessed with the way that she thought about lyrics and how thoughtful she was with the arrangement of the song.

Now that she has broken through, Dan could not be more delighted for her, telling MBW, 'It feels really incredible because we've been working at it for so long. We were trying to push through a certain wall and now we've got through, so that's as good as it gets.'

Speaking about what draws him to an artist, he says he asks himself, do they have an interesting song topic, and can you hear that conviction and intensity in the voice?

And believing that his own strongest suit is chords and melody, he enjoys working with artists like Olivia and Chappell who are lyric driven, describing the connection as 'like finding puzzle pieces that fit together'.

Chappell Roan, Justin Tranter, and Dan Nigro at the 67th Annual GRAMMY Awards, Los Angeles, 2025

Chappell described their songwriting process in a Radio 1 podcast, saying, 'We listen to a lot of different songs that are inspiring us, try different beats, we sometimes come with a concept'.

Chappell chat

'Dan always believed in me. He has been there from the beginning and brought me into realising what makes me feel good to perform, what makes me feel good to sing, to write about. Because he believed in bringing that part of myself to life, I started to believe in it, too.'

Speaking to The New York Times.

Believing in her talent, and committed to providing the creative freedom she needed, Dan stuck with Chappell through the highs and lows of her rise to fame.

'I've always known that Chappell was a great live performer even before she was playing shows, with how good she was on the microphone and how much she could control her voice,' Dan told *MBW*. 'You just knew she was going to be able to do something special onstage.'

It was through Dan that Chappell connected with Olivia and got to sing as a backing singer on a few of her tracks. Then after Midwest Princess came out, Chappell began opening shows for Olivia on her *Guts* arena tour.

'I think the age gap and generation gap work to our advantage because Dan and I come from different perspectives on music and culture,' Chappell has said of their relationship. 'It only strengthens the world that we build.'

Chappell Attending the premiere of Netflix's *Olivia Rodrigo: GUTS World Tour* at NYA East, Los Angeles, 2024

Mike Wise

Mike Wise is a multifaceted music producer and songwriter who has worked with Dan and Chappell on several tracks.

Growing up in Toronto, Canada, Wise was immersed in a rich musical environment where early exposure to various genres, from rock and pop to hip-hop and electronic music, laid the foundation for his career as a top tier producer. As well as Chappell, Mike has worked with Ellie Goulding, Leah Kate and James Blunt, each time bringing his unique touch to their music.

His production style is characterised by a keen attention to detail, a deep understanding of musical dynamics, and a talent for enhancing the emotional impact of a song.

Ellie Goulding performs on stage during the BRIT Awards 2024 at The 02 Arena on March 02, 2024 in London, England.

Ryan Linvill

Another sought after musician who has come in to support Dan and Chappell is songwriter/producer Ryan Linvill, who has worked in genres from pop and indie to electronic and hip-hop. His ability to blend traditional musical elements with modern production techniques so seamlessly has become a hallmark of his work.

His collaboration with Chappell has been particularly fruitful, resulting in a series of acclaimed tracks that highlight both Roan's vocal prowess and Linvill's innovative production. Their work together began to receive attention with the release of *California*, which showcased Linvill's knack for creating lush, atmospheric soundscapes that perfectly complement Chappell's emotive singing style.

Chappell's super graphic ultra-modern look

Chapter 5

Chappell's super graphic ultra-modern look

Chappell chat

'I pretty much base my aesthetic off what a pop star would have worn when I was 8. When I was little, I loved Bratz, the classic Barbie movies, Britney Spears, I was really into fairies and Spy Kids.'

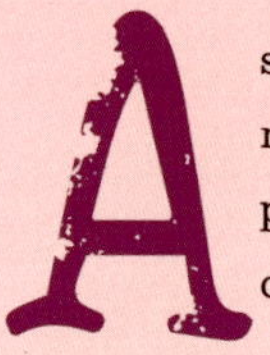

As the 'new face' in pop music, Chappell tried a new face herself. She started by painting her face pure white, then added red lips to match her red curly hair.

'I started to do that because that's what the country boys called gay people in my hometown. Clowns. Like, they were really embarrassing, like clowns, they danced like clowns,' she told singer and drag queen Trixie Mattel in an interview for *Paper*.

'I was just like, I'll show you a clown, if you want to see a clown! So I started doing that and also referencing the girls in the '20s, all the classic stuff. Also my blue eyeshadow, I always love blue eyeshadow and a big red lip, glitter, my favs'.

Chappell chat

'The whole project is to honour my 10-year-old self. My whole persona is just me trying to honour that version of myself that I was never allowed to be.'

'I want to purposely look "trashy," not modest, very loud and provocative', she told *Cherwell* in 2022. 'To me that is a reflection of and an homage to burlesque. It's consciously camp. Because I was not allowed to express that kind of showmanship in Missouri where I'm from, the pendulum has swung so far the other way. I don't think I would have been as outgoing and obnoxious if I had been from the coasts.'

The heavily made up look then morphed into something more drag-influenced following Chappell's interactions with the drag community.

Chappell Attending the premiere of Netflix's *Olivia Rodrigo: GUTS World Tour* at NYA East, Los Angeles, 2024

Chappell chat

'When I was Kayleigh Rose, I was performing all over town in coffee shops in Springfield, Missouri and I was very modest,' 'I always wore knee-length dresses and very high necks. Nothing like what I would wear now.'

Speaking during a 2022 pre-mega-fame interview with Cherwell - the student magazine of Oxford University.

She was first exposed to drag when her uncle, a gay man, took her to a drag show featuring brunch and bingo. 'I was like, oh god this is so fun,' said Chappell. 'I became obsessed with the fashion and the makeup and the performance and just the silliness of the whole thing. It was just so unserious and that is where I latch on to today – you do not need to take this seriously, it's just pop music, you know.'

Even before she was famous, Chappell began to get drag queens to open her shows – something she still does today - and, when in London she had a conversation with a queen called Crayola which really changed her whole performance trajectory. As Chappell explained to Tom Power on the *Q* entertainment podcast, Crayola told her that she (Chappell) was herself a drag queen.

Drag queen Donna Trump Serving glamour under the stage lights with feathers, florals and voluminous locks

Roan rocking the stage at the Bonnaroo Music and Arts Festival, Manchester, Tennessee, 2024

'I was just getting ready and my makeup wasn't done yet and I said to her, oh I'm like you, I need to get my makeup and my clothes on and kind of transform and she was like, "Honey, you are a drag queen, you are not just getting makeup on, you are a drag queen" and I was like oh my god. That was very altering, there was something that switched over the summer after I did that and I really have taken that on as an identity and it's been very freeing. Chappell Roan is my drag project and it's also helped personally to separate it as a job and there is me as Kayleigh. It's a useful way of framing it so there's distance between who you really are.'

Ever since then Chappell's representation of the drag community has been incredible and positive. She has given hope to many young people by making her concerts into celebrations of queerness and drag.

And in return the drag artistry has helped Chappell to develop her music and performance style.

She's convinced that her music would not sound the same if she had not encountered the drag community when she did, believing she would be 'boring'.

Crayola

Crayola the Queen is the alter ego of actor Gigi Zahir (Nominated Best Host, QX 2019) a London-based singer, comedian and MC.

ayola's "The Life-Cycle a Drag Gig" Instagram post, 2024

Chappell chat

No one performs better than a drag queen. And I stand behind that. They push me to go bigger with my outfits, go bolder with my lyrics, just really let go when it comes to performing on stage, dancing, the 'campiness', just the humour, behind pop music and behind drag are very similar. Drag queens are my biggest inspiration, and burlesque dancers, just any kind of hypnotising, outrageous spectacle.'

Some people were confused about how a woman could be a drag queen, but drag now covers any art form that pivots upon a put on effect, an alternate identity. This means that cisgender women can do female-presenting drag, as Chappell does.

Positive proof of her impact came when Chappell was honoured at the 2024 Output100 as a 'disruptor' and also praised by her 'mother' Sasha Colby, winner of RuPaul's Drag Race season 15.

'Chappell Roan's music is a bold, vulnerable, yet fearless expression of unapologetic authenticity and true talent,' Sasha told *Out* magazine. '...serving as a reminder that the voices and stories of the LGBTQ+ community inspire us all to live courageously and unapologetically'.

Chappell wows in a pink and blue wrestling-inspired ensemble, delivering an electrifying performance on Day 1 of Lollapalooza, Chicago, 2024

Through various different interviews, performances, references, and connections, Chappell immersed herself in queer culture, drag, burlesque and cabaret as she grew her career as a pop star. Yet it wasn't until June 2024 that Chappell confirmed she identified as a lesbian.

Chappell Roan attends the 2024 MTV Video Music Awards at UBS Arena on September 11, 2024 in Elmont, New York.

Visionary styling

LA-based stylist and creative director Genesis Webb has worked with Chappell on her most arresting looks.

The two women met on a shoot for *V* magazine and bonded immediately over a shared passion for vintage clothing. They then discovered they shared similar small town upbringings – Chappell coming from Missouri and Genesis from Oklahoma.

Already a leading force in contemporary fashion, with her disruptive ideas featured in *Vogue*, *New York Times*, *Paper*, *NME*, and *Billboard*, Genesis has been challenged in new ways since she began collaborating with Chappell during her rise to fame.

Speaking about her work with Genesis, Chappell said, '... we pull from drag, we pull from horror movies, we pull from burlesque, we pull from theatre...I love looking pretty and scary or tacky, or just not pretty, I love that too. It's not serious.'

'She wants to go as big as possible,' Genesis has said of working with Chappell. 'If you're not pushing something, then why are we doing it at all?'

'Pushing it' has included the two swan outfits Genesis created for Chappell to wear during her key appearance on The Tonight Show with Jimmy Fallon. For the sit-down interview section Genesis dressed Chappell in a black mini dress adorned with massive feather plumes, then for her performance of *Good Luck, Babe!* she changed into a white version of a swan costume, with a heavily feathered headpiece, sleeves and hem.

The overall look was enhanced by makeup artist Andrew Dahling' who gave Chappell bold black and white eye makeup - eyelashes exaggerated by ghostly, white feathers - and even more feathers on her hands.

While Chappell understands the interest in her look, she sometimes finds it frustrating, once saying, 'No one's out there asking Bieber *how does your fashion move feminism forward*?'

Chappell chat

'Nothing turns me off more than **frickin' luxury brands**'.

As Chappell's stages and audiences have got bigger, so have the outfit ideas from Genesis. Recent headline-grabbing looks have included a hot pink prom dress for her NPR Tiny Desk performance and the Statue of Liberty-look Chappell wore for her performance at the Governors Ball music festival.

Her Statue of Liberty makeup, again by Andrew Dahling, included painting her body in two layers of green paint, all over, which took more than four hours.

'To a normal person, the extremity of it, the pain and the inconvenience of it all would have just been annoying," Andrew said. Not so for Chappell and her styling team. 'Whatever it takes to get the look, we're into it,' said Andrew.

Roan commands the stage at the Governors Ball in her reimagined take on the Statue of Liberty, 2024

Chappell's super graphic ultra-modern look

Chat about Chappell

Olivia Rodrigo

'She [Chappell] deserves it all'

Chat about Chappell

Dan Nigro

'I've always known that Chappell was a great live performer even before she was playing shows; with how good she was on the microphone and how much she could control her voice, you just knew she was going to be able to do something special on stage. It's amazing for fans that get to experience such a great live performer.'

Elton John

'Your album is doing so brilliantly.... I'm as excited about your album's success as you are. It's wonderful to see true talent being recognized,'

Speaking to Chappell on his Apple Music radio show, Rocket Hour

SexyTadhg

(Irish singer and drag performer)

'For a long time, queer artists have always felt the need to either take out information so that people don't know that their songs are about the queer experience, or maybe they change pronouns to make it more palatable for a mainstream audience. The fact that Chappell hasn't dulled or diminished her story, and is still incredibly successful, is so inspiring.'

Nick Bobetsky

Chappell Roan's manager

'What I saw, straight away, was already a next-level talent, and a level of confidence, even at that stage of her career, that was truly remarkable.

'She had a conviction about who she was that was unshakeable. She's wired in such a way that when you meet her, you realise, she's just got it. She was still only 19, but it was clear to me that Chappell was going to be an artist that really mattered for a long time.'

Speaking to Music Business Worldwide, August 2024.

Donna Fella

from drag trio Haus of Wig, who opened for Chappell in Dublin 2024.

'The way in which she's risen is very unique and doesn't happen all the time. I think that forming a community and having such a strong identity – in terms of handling and expressing your art, on your own terms – is very empowering, especially for queer artists.'

Shaqira Knightly,

Haus of Wig,

'I think she strikes a chord because there's something very fresh about her sound, something very unapologetic and a bit uncharted,'.

The Rise and Fall of a Midwest Princess

The Rise and Fall of a Midwest Princess

Chapter 6

In September 2023, six years after putting out her *School Nights* EP, Chappell released her debut album, *The Rise and Fall of a Midwest Princess*.

Audacious and roisterous, it was a bold debut which won widespread acclaim, appearing in all the year-end best album lists including those published by *Vogue*, *Rolling Stone*, *TIME* and *Billboard*. Pitchfork's review said the album was 'buoyed by sturdy songcraft and steely indifference to good taste'. It was nominated for Album of the Year at the 2025 Grammy awards.

At first, public reaction was muted as it remained a niche favourite among the queer community. But as more and more people got the chance to hear it when Chappell began opening for Olivia Rodrigo on her Guts tour, the buzz around it steadily grew.

Chappell Roan shimmers on stage under the neon glow of her name at Rodrigo's *GUTS World Tour*, 2024

As people started to see her as well as hear her, Chappell became instantly recognisable for her makeup and staging. Interviewed by the UK's BBC Radio 1 she explained how she was aligning her appearance with drag culture and the 'outrageous spectacle' that it is.

In an interview with the *Vulture* website, Chappell described her songs as really coming into their own once she 'stopped trying to impress the music industry and started trying to impress gay people'.

Poses for a portrait in her dressing room at the House of Blues in Chicago, IL, on Thursday, October 5, 2023

Evidencing her excitement around the visual element of her Chappell Roan persona, she also said that 'The only Grammy I want to win is album packaging' referencing her album cover which was heavily inspired by the burlesque and drag cultures which she loves.

She was keen to make clear that she discovered her own queerness while making the album, saying that a lot of it came from daydreams and fantasising – concluding that 'the creative world building was really what realised my queer identity'.

In changing her identity, Chappell also changed her music. The sound of the songs on *The Rise and Fall of a Midwest Princess* was drastically different from her original material and much more evolved.

'I wanted to make an album that I could party to, and other people could party to', said Chappell. 'And so I would never be sad or bored performing because I think that's why I changed to pure pop. It would be so boring, performing sad songs all the time.'

The Rise and Fall of a Midwest Princess

Track Listing

- ***Femininomenon***
- ***Red Wine Supernova***
- ***After Midnight***
- ***Coffee***
- ***Casual***
- ***Super Graphic Ultra Modern Girl***
- ***HOT TO GO!***
- ***My Kink is Karma***
- ***Picture You***
- ***Kaleidoscope***
- ***Pink Pony Club***
- ***Naked in Manhattan***
- ***California***
- ***Guilty Pleasure***

Track by track

Femininomenon (3.39)

This rousing call and response anthem leads the charge for a cultural shift towards women's empowerment, powered by Chappell's bold lyrics and Dan Nigro's vibrant production.

Released on 12 August 2022, *Femininomenon* was the fifth single from the album and was produced by Dan Nigro and Mike Wise. Chappell and Dan reportedly wrote sections on different days and pieced them together. Similarly, the title is a portmanteau of the words feminine and phenomenon.

In an interview with online music magazine *Earmilk*, Chappell said, 'I've been dreaming of releasing a song like this my whole career. It took years to build up the confidence to even sing in that style. I always try to push myself and how I write pop music. I want to see if I can get away with being as ridiculous as I possibly can. I wanted a dance song. Something people could do drag to. A queer anthem that had a sad undertone of what really happened to me, but with a beat.'

Speaking to *Cherwell* magazine, Chappell said the song was the confusion she had in relation to her sexual relationships with men. 'Something is not connecting. I feel like every man I've been

Chappell lights up the stage at the 2024 Austin City Limits Music Festival in Zilker Park, Austin, Texas

with is never satisfying. With a woman, it's easy and different and wonderful. It's a phenomenon. It's a queer song – hidden in there... It's a phenomenon that this magical, perfect scenario somewhere out there exists, and it's probably a woman in my case.'

Emily Treadgold of *Earmilk* said that 'the song somehow goes in a million different ways but fits together so well and is so fun and loud but so intricate'.

As part of his review of the album for AllMusic, Neil Z. Yeung said that the song 'perfectly captures the album's ethos as it transforms from a sweet, string-laden ballad into a pulse-pounding empowerment anthem punctuated by a mid-song pep talk and hilariously escalating adlibs'.

Cover art for *Red Wine Supernova*

Red Wine Supernova (3.12)

Red Wine Supernova is a shining example of Chappell's talents as she delves into the exhilarating and liberating experience of a queer hookup, seen through the lens of carefree drunkenness. The song's 'supernova' moment imagines a world where nothing else matters, inviting listeners to either imagine or remember the intoxicating thrill of first love. With vivid storytelling and a euphoric melody, the track celebrates the joy that defines falling in love for the first time. Music and entertainment news source *Pop Crave* placed it #14 in its Top 20 Pop Songs of 2023 list, *Rolling Stone* placed it #18 and NME put it at #47. Chappell herself has described the track as the 'gay-girl' version of *Champagne Supernova* by 90s Britpop band Oasis.

Chappell Roan kicks off her UK and European *The Midwest Princess Tour* with a performance at Manchester Academy, UK, 2024

After Midnight (3.24)

Speaking on Tom Power's *Q* podcast, Chappell said that this song was inspired by her dad who always said, '...nothing good happens after midnight', whereas in fact everything I remember and made me feel good happened after midnight!

'Anyway it's just bubble gum and made me feel good...I wanted something fluffy.'

Chappell Roan performs on stage at FirstBank Amphitheater in Franklin, Tennessee, during *The Midwest Princess Tour*, October, 2024

Coffee (3.25)

Exploring the emotional complexities of navigating a complicated romantic relationship, Chappell sings about struggling to find neutral territory to meet for a coffee – somewhere unlikely to reignite past conflicts or emotional turmoil.

The idea of meeting for coffee symbolises an attempt to keep things simple and avoid deeper entanglements that could arise from meeting in more intimate or alcohol-influenced settings. Although in the end the whole plan is abandoned as too fraught, wherever the setting.

Her vocal delivery is particularly powerful on this track, while still managing to show tenderness and vulnerability.

Casual (3.52)

This song is the ying to the yang of *Red Wine Supernova*. While in the second song she celebrates the fun of strings-free hook ups, in *Casual*, she laments any such lack of romanticism and yearns for commitment.

Both songs employ viscerally sexual lyrics, although as Chappell told the Los Angeles Times, '... I was dating a boy ...I had never even kissed a girl when these songs were written. It was all what I wished my life could be.'

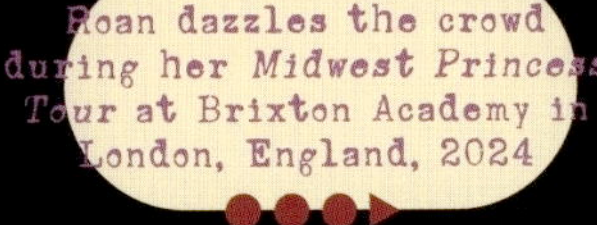
Roan dazzles the crowd during her *Midwest Princess Tour* at Brixton Academy in London, England, 2024

Super Graphic Ultra Modern Girl (3.03)

This vibrant, high-energy pop song delves into themes of self-discovery and transformation and celebrates the experience of falling in queer love for the first time. Chappell describes a fantastical place where women thrive without men, enjoying the subsequent freedom and empowerment. Critics have described it as a technicolour celebration, with elements that evoke the fun and eccentric style of the B-52s.

The song and its accompanying music video have been praised for their bold, expressive style and infectious energy. Critics have highlighted Chappell's ability to blend fun pop hooks with deeper messages about identity and sexuality.

Chappell Roan takes over the Lands End stage at the 2024 Outside Lands Music and Arts Festival in Golden Gate Park, San Francisco, 2024

HOT TO GO! (3.04)

HOT TO GO! is a 'cheer' song with a fun dance attached to it. Chappell is said to have been inspired to write her own banger by watching clips of the iconic and theatrical British rock band Queen interacting with the crowd clapping along to their 1984 hit *Radio Gaga*.

Describing the writing process with Dan Nigro on this track, Chappell told the Radio 1 Podcast interview; 'I walked in and said I need something that is like my version of YMCA where I can do a dance with the audience. I'm a huge fan of audience participation. So with that in mind we looked up cheerleading chants and we wrote that song super-fast because I knew exactly what I wanted and how it was going to sound.'

Continuing to outline her writing process, Chappell said, 'When it comes to upbeat pop music, anthemic bubbly pop, then I'm Chappell. But when it comes to your ballads it's much easier to write from Kayleigh's perspective just because that's how I feel myself, not as my drag persona. It's just like the drag persona is much more exhausting to portray in the writing sense. It's two different worlds that come into one, the heavy personal part and then these anthemic pop songs which really turn a lot of labels off me, which is why I got dropped. A lot of people did not understand it ... to have both sides of the same coin to be represented in an album ... but obviously now we see that it's working, but it's hard to balance it.'

Chappell Roan performs her signature *Hot To Go!* dance

My Kink is Karma (3.42)

This sincere song is about negotiating the emotional trauma and upheaval of a break-up, but with humour. Chappell has said of the song, 'Dan, my main co-writer and producer, and I always try not to take every song too seriously. I think humour in pop music is great. Lizzo is amazing at that. Gaga is interesting because her camp is serious – *Born This Way* puts out an important message but still has a laugh behind it. I haven't gotten to that point, but I'd like to get there. I think right now I'm in the humour category because I don't know how to explore camp in a serious way. *My Kink is Karma* is purposely outrageous and funny. I want it to be fun and ridiculous.

Picture You (3.07)

Chappell has performed this torch song about unrequited obsession by serenading a wig set on top of a microphone stand.

Delving into themes of longing and unspoken desire, Chappell imagines intimate moments with someone she cares about, and feelings which she is too scared to express openly. Lines like, 'I'm too scared to say, half of the things I do when I picture you' capture this internal conflict between fantasy and reality.

Kaleidoscope (3.42)

Kaleidoscope delves into the emotions of falling in love with a best friend, the complex feelings of unrequited love, and the shift from platonic to romantic affection. Chappell has shared that the song is based on her personal experience of falling for her best friend, which was both a beautiful and challenging period in her life.

Speaking to *Pop Crave* in February 2023, Chappell said that *Kaleidoscope* was currently the favourite song she had ever written. Compared to her purer pop numbers, this veers towards balladry, with a lush and minimalistic arrangement using strings and cyclical piano progression to underline the song's introspective nature.

Performance at the 2024 Bonnaroo Music and Arts Festival in Manchester, Tennessee, 2024

Pink Pony Club (4.18)

One of Chappell's most popular songs, the *Pink Pony Club* track tells the story of a girl from the Midwest finding friends and a safe space in a gay club in Los Angeles. It's an anthem of self-acceptance which has emboldened many a young queer woman. (And see chapter four.)

Naked in Manhattan (3.31)

Naked in Manhattan is the second of two songs Chappell wrote about queer relationships before she had even kissed a girl in real life (the second being *Red Wine Supernova*). 'I was dating a boy when I wrote it. It was all that I wished my life could be,' she told *The Los Angeles Times*. It was her first explicitly queer track, given that *Pink Pony Club* was deliberately ambiguous and open to interpretation.

The 02 Academy Brixton in London, where Chappell Roan performs for three nights during her *Midwest Princess Tour*, 2024

A sea of Chappell fans in their signature cowboy hats

Live on stage during *The Midwest Princess Tour* at Manchester Academy in Manchester, England, 2024

California (3.18)

This is another of Chappell's earliest songs on this album, having been written and released on 29 May 2020 while she was still signed to Atlantic.

She's honest and relatable as she sings about the homesickness she experienced after moving from her home state of Missouri to California in pursuit of her dreams. It reflects on the struggles associated with major life changes, the discomfort of being in a new place, and missing the comfort and simplicity of home.

Guilty Pleasure (3.44)

The song reflects Chappell's personal journey coming to terms with her queer identity, as she explores the theme of indulging in something that feels forbidden or taboo.

It features eclectic musical shifts and unconventional elements, such as a dramatic key change and a yodelling bridge, making it a stand-out, bold and experimental track. Critics have praised Guilty Pleasure for its unique structure and Roan's willingness to push boundaries within the pop genre.

Chappell chat

'I was like... 'is this even good'?, - just kidding I knew it was good. I was actually surprised by critical acclaim but thought, the girls are gonna love this. If I didn't think it was good I wouldn't have put it out.'

Chappell performs at Revolution Live in Fort Lauderdale, Florida during *The Midwest Princess Tour*, 2023

The crowd goes wild during Chappell Roan's set at the Capitol Hill Block Party in Seattle, 2024

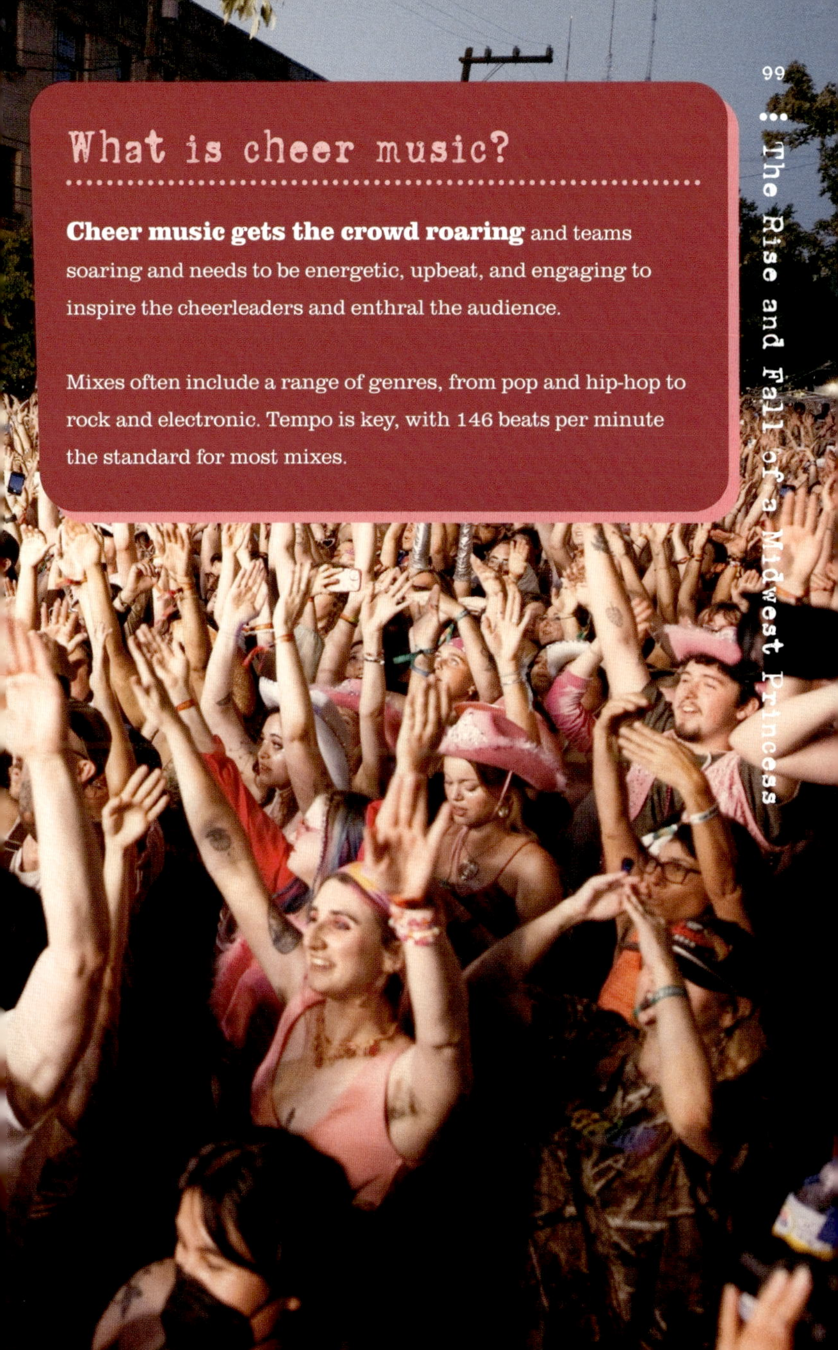

What is cheer music?

Cheer music gets the crowd roaring and teams soaring and needs to be energetic, upbeat, and engaging to inspire the cheerleaders and enthral the audience.

Mixes often include a range of genres, from pop and hip-hop to rock and electronic. Tempo is key, with 146 beats per minute the standard for most mixes.

Partying on tour

Chapter 7

Fans get to experience something special at a Chappell Roan concert – she's such a great live performer. As headliner at last, she had the chance to perform exactly as she wanted to for the first time. And she knew exactly what she wanted - to make sure that every single one of her shows was a party.

Echoing the title of her hit song *Naked in Manhattan*, Chappell's first headlining tour was called *Naked In North America*. It ran from February to March 2023 comprising 20 sold-out gigs.

Each concert had its own dress up theme for the crowd, an idea which she was trying out and has since adopted wholesale. She also tried an idea from fellow queer artist Orville Peck in getting local drag queens as her opening act.

'It's a really great way to engage the local queer community to that city,' Chappell told People magazine in September 2023. "I encourage people to tip the queens, that's redistributing funds within the community there, and also it just gives a platform for the drag queens. Some of these queens have never performed in front of a crowd that big before, and it's just fun.'

Interviewed by *Pop Crave,* she said the feeling of headlining was 'surreal' adding 'Regardless of anything I just want to create a fun place for people – especially queer people to feel safe, dress up and know that they're not gonna be judged. It's a very communal vibe.'

Shanika Sunrise supports Chappell during *The Midwest Princess Tour* at Mancheter Academy, Manchester, UK, 2024

Pearl

Expanding on the idea behind her 'themed' nights, Chappell said, 'I just wanted something that gave people an option to dress up, because I love dressing up all crazy. It gives you the option and a comfortability around dressing how you would on Halloween, honestly, because everyone else is doing it with you. No one's gonna think you're weird! It's just an opportunity to be silly, honestly. That's my whole thing.'

Fans dressed up and ready for Roan's show at the House of Blues in Chicago, 2023

Her suggestions to fans have included pink cowgirl dress for *Pink Pony Girl* themed concerts, slumber party looks for *Naked in Manhattan* nights and black and red (or anything that makes you feel hot) for *My Kink is Karma*.

'I've always wanted to do themed shows because I love crowd participation. Like that is my thing. I write songs with the intention of the crowd participating in them,' says Chappell.

'She's really thoughtful about the experience for fans," said her tour manager, Nick Bobetsky. '...especially venue selection, parts of town, gender-neutral bathrooms, like really creating a safe space, making sure that we prep building security on, you know, that there's a large queer young community coming to this.'

Chappell Roan at Coachella, 2024

Speaking to *Glamour* magazine in May 2023, Chappell said; 'We had three local drag performers from every city that we did. The themes were based off of my songs or things that were in my world, so I really was like, "How do I dress up as Hannah Montana? Oh, pop star theme because I love Hannah. And I grew up with her." We had a "Pink Pony Club" theme, we had a "My Kink Is Karma" theme. We had Rainbow Night, Goth Night; it was super fun. I wanted it to feel different and fun. And it was really f***ing hard. I feel like it broke me a little bit mentally, because of how emotionally draining it was, but fulfilling at the same time. Touring is hard. Especially in a van. It was worth it because of how fulfilling it was emotionally, but physically, it was just so crazy and hard.'

Chappell's performance energy is off the scale. It takes weeks for her to build up and maintain the stamina she needs to belt out her songs while jogging along and without missing a beat. She has said that she takes two months of cardio vocal training, on top of HITT work outs and rope jumping so that 'I finally don't feel like I'm gonna throw up when I sing', as she told her Insta followers.

Her shows were so packed with shareable moments – like the choreography from HOT TO GO! and the themed dress up opportunities – that clips from her performance deluged short-form video platforms like Tik Tok.

Throughout her show, key phrases from her songs are displayed on a video screen so that the crowd can sing along.

A supporting role

Although Chappell didn't get to headline her own tour until 2023, she had played supporting roles in other artist's tours before, including opening for Vance Joy, Ben Platt, Fletcher and Declan McKenna.

But the biggest of all the stars she opened for was her Nigro stablemate Olivia Rodrigo. Talking about the honour of opening for Olivia she told ABC News, 'I had never played an arena before and it was scary to think there's 20,000 people out there, though you can't see past the first 1000.'

After meeting Olivia through Dan Nigro, Chappell worked briefly on Olivia's 2022 'Sour' tour. Chappell also provided some backing vocals for Olivia's second album *Guts*, *on Lacy*, *Obsessed* and *Bad Idea*, *Right*, after which she was asked to open for Olivia on her 'Guts' tour from February to April 2024.

It was during these American concerts that Chappell's career began to explode and enter the mainstream. Everything had come together at last – she had gained agency and grown in confidence, found the drag influenced style that suited her – and of course had a collection of relatable tracks which were more emotional and sexually frank. She had learned through her earlier failure and rather than beat herself up about it, had used the experience to evolve and find the opportunities in it.

Chappell chat

'A solid, sold-out headline tour with this project is my goal. I want to play the album all over the place. I would love to go on an international tour. I would love to take it to the UK. I want to release amazing, fun merch and videos around it. I want to build this little world that I've always imagined and share it with everyone.'

Speaking to Cherwell magazine in 2022.

Chappell Roan and Olivia Rodrigo perform at Olivia's *GUTS World Tour*, Los Angeles, 2024

2023 Naked in North America tour

Dates

FEBRUARY 2023

15 ***Crescent Ballroom, Phoenix, Arizona, USA***

18 ***House of Blues (Cambridge Room) Dallas, Texas, USA***

19 ***House of Blues (Bronze Peacock) Houston, Texas, USA***

20 ***The Parish, Austin, Texas, USA***

22 ***Vinyl, Atlanta, Georgia, USA***

23 ***Basement East, Nashville, Tennessee, USA***

25 ***Foundry at The Fillmore, Philadelphia, Pennsylvania, USA***

26 ***Black Cat, Washington DC, USA***

28 ***Webster Hall, New York, New York, USA***

Chappell live at FirstBank Amphitheater in Franklin, Tennessee, for *The Midwest Princess Tour*, 2024

MARCH 2023

1	Sinclair, Boston, Massachusetts, USA
3	Velvet Underground, Toronto, Ontario, Canada
4	A&R Music Bar, Columbus, Ohio, USA
5	Subterranean, Chicago, Illinois, USA
6	Gillioz Theatre, Springfield, Missouri, USA
8	Marquis Theatre, Denver, Colorado, USA
9	Soundwell, Salt Lake City, Utah, USA
11	Madame Lou's, Seattle, Washington, USA
12	Doug Fir Lounge, Portland, Oregon, USA
14	August Hall, San Francisco, California, USA
15	The Fonda Theatre, Los Angeles, California, USA

Chappell's second headlining tour was bigger and better than anything she had done before. Called 'The Midwest Princess Tour', and in support of her debut album, *The Rise and Fall of a Midwest Princess*, it ran for 89 shows from September 2023 to October 2024 throughout America and Europe.

During those 13 months Chappell's career took off to such an extent that venues booked early on were far too small to house her swelling audiences by the time she got to them.

Her first date was in a venue which held 600 people. By the time she got to Seattle nine months later she performed to a crown of 10,000, and by now even that venue is too small for her. Fans were lucky to see her at close quarters, as her next concerts are sure to be in stadiums and arenas.

Chappell performs at Boston Calling, 2024

2023 The Midwest Princess tour

Dates

SEPTEMBER 2023

20 Gillioz Theatre, Springfield, Missouri, USA

25 Goldfield Trading Company, Roseville, Sacramento, USA

27 The Depot, Salt Lake City, USA

29 Ogden Theatre, Denver, USA

OCTOBER 2023

1 First Avenue, Minneapolis, USA

3 The Rave/Eagles Club, Milwaukee, USA

4/5 House of Blues, Chicago, USA

7 Brooklyn Bowl, Nashville, USA

8 Old National Centre, Indianapolis, USA

10 Saint Andrew's Hall, Detroit, USA

11 The Opera House, Toronto, Canada

12 Théâtre Fairmount, Montreal, Canada

14 The Fillmore, Philadelphia, USA

15 House of Blues, Boston, USA

17/18 Brooklyn Steel, Brooklyn, NYC, USA

20/21 9:30 Club, Washington, D.C., USA

22 The Underground, Charlotte, USA

24 Buckhead Theatre, Atlanta, USA

Roan brings her energy to Red Hat Amphitheater in Raleigh, N.C, 2024

Serving *Midwest Princess* magic on stage at FirstBank Amphitheater in Franklin, Tennessee, 2024

OCTOBER 2023 continued...

25 Beacham Theatre, Orlando, USA

26 Revolution Live, Fort Lauderdale, USA

28 Joy Theatre, New Orleans, USA

29 House of Blues, Houston, Texas, USA

31 House of Blues, Dallas, Texas, USA

NOVEMBER 2023

1 Scoot Inn, Austin, Texas, USA

3 The Van Buren, Phoenix, Arizona, USA

4 24 Oxford at the Virgin Hotels, Las Vegas, USA

7 UC Theatre, Berkeley, California, USA

9 Wonder Ballroom, Portland, Oregon, USA

10 Hollywood Theatre, Vancouver, Canada

11 The Showbox, Seattle, USA

14 The Wiltern, Los Angeles, USA

Oceania

24 Liberty Hall, Sydney, Australia

25 Brisbane Powerhouse, Brisbane, Australia

26 170 Russell, Melbourne, Australia

DECEMBER 2023

3 FRANNZ Club, Berlin, Germany

5 Melkweg OZ, Amsterdam, Netherlands

6 Les Étoiles, Paris, France

7/8 Heaven, London, England

MARCH 2024

17 Val Air Ballroom, Des Moines, Iowa, USA

25 Higher Ground Ballroom, South Burlington, Vermont, USA

APRIL 2024

3 College Street Music Hall, New Haven, Connecticut, USA

5 Stage AE, Pittsburgh, USA

6 The Intersection, Grand Rapids, Michigan, USA

8 Midland Theatre, Kansas City, USA

9 Boulder Theatre, Boulder, Colorado, USA

12/19 Empire Polo Club, Indio, California, USA

MAY 2024

17 The Hangout, Gulf Shores, Alabama, USA

19 Jannus Live, St Petersburg, Florida, USA

20 Firefly Distillery, North Charleston, South Carolina, USA

22 Rabbit Rabbit, Asheville, North Carolina, USA

23 Brown's Island, Richmond, Virginia, USA

24 Terminal B at the Outer Harbor, Buffalo, New York, USA

26 Harvard Athletic Complex, Boston, USA

28 Jacobs Pavilion, Cleveland, Ohio, USA

29 The Sylvee, Madison, Wisconsin, USA

30 Saint Louis Music Park, Maryland Heights, Missouri, USA

Chappell fans basking in the glow of pink lights and feeling the *Midwest Princess* energy

JUNE

1 State Theatre, Kalamazoo, Michigan, USA

4 Little Rock Hall, Little Rock, Arkansas ,USA

5 Cain's Ballroom, Tulsa, Oklahoma, USA

7 KEMBA live!, Columbus, Ohio, USA'

9 Flushing Meadows – Corona Park, New York, USA

11 The NorVa, Norfolk, Virginia, USA

12 Red Hat Amphitheatre, Raleigh, North Carolina, USA

13 Columbia Township Auditorium, Columbia, South Carolina, USA

15 Big 4 Lawn, Louisville, Kentucky, USA

16 Great Stage Park, Manchester, New Hampshire, USA

19 Capitol Hill, Seattle, Washington, USA

31 The Vic Theatre, Chicago, USA

Live on stage at Manchester Academy in Manchester, England, 2024

Chappell performs at FirstBank Amphitheater in Franklin, Tennessee, 2024

AUGUST

1 Grant Park, Chicago, USA

2 Parc Jean-Drapeau, Montreal, Canada,

4 Avenue of the Saints Amphitheatre, St Charles, Missouri, USA

11 Golden Gate Park, San Francisco, USA

SEPTEMBER

13 Manchester Academy, Manchester, England, UK

15 O2 Academy, Glasgow, Scotland, UK

17 Olympia Theatre, Dublin, Ireland

19/20/21 O2 Academy, Brixton, London, UK

23 The Velodrome, Berlin, Germany

OCTOBER

1 FirstBank Amphitheater, Franklin, Indiana, USA

2 Walmart AMP, Rogers, Arkansas, USA

3 Westfair Amphitheater, Council Bluffs, Iowa, USA

6/13 Zilker Park, Austin, Texas, USA

Good Luck, Babe!

Good Luck, Babe!

Chapter 8

In 2024 Chappell became one of the biggest pop stars in the world, with sell-out shows, millions of streams and a huge and devoted fan base. The fact that just a few years earlier she was back living with her parents in Missouri and selling coffee seems unbelievable.

After 'breathing' for a year, in June 2024, *The Rise and Fall of a Midwest Princess* and many of its singles dominated the charts and made #1 on iTunes. She had three singles in the Billboard Top 100, while the album went to #1 in the UK and New Zealand, #2 in America (#1 on US iTunes chart) and the Netherlands, and #3 in Australia. Chappell's music was boosted by some truly outstanding performances at the leading festivals of the summer, and her new single *Good Luck, Babe!* which became the defining single of the summer (and was nominated as such at the 2024 VMAs). It was nominated as Record of the Year and Song of the Year at the 2025 Grammys.

This song, about the complexity of heterosexual relationships and the self-denial sometimes involved, introduced her new, wider and more mainstream audience to a queer narrative. Within weeks it amassed 200m streams on Spotify, boosting her overall numbers from two million to 21 million monthly listeners. By September 2024 she had 45 million monthly listeners.

Chappell was everything, everywhere, all at once – leaving no one in any doubt that this was absolutely her moment.

Chappell Roan at the UMG GRAMMY After Party, Los Angeles, 2024

Good Luck, Babe!

This synth-driven banger shot up the charts when it was released in April 2024 as a standalone single through Amusement Records and Island Records, giving Chappell her first big hit on the Billboard Hot 100. Written with Justin Tranter and the song's producer Dan Nigro, it has an explicitly queer narrative, telling the story of a gay love affair which ends with the ex-lover leaving her female partner and trying to get over their affair by kissing 'a hundred boys in bars' before eventually marrying a man and living unhappily ever after.

Chappell was very happy when she evoked comparisons with singer Kate Bush, who first found fame in the late 1970s, particularly around the vocal trills and almighty wailing both have employed in their singing. 'I am obsessed with Kate Bush and the way she is so fully free in her vocal approach', she told the Radio 1 Podcast Interview. 'Like so weird in the best way possible and that's what inspires me. I don't need to be this slick pop voice. I can be like Kate Bush - a mixture of theatre and opera, and pop. I'd love to embody her energy and her fearlessness'.

Kate Bush, 1985

Its success brought her into the mainstream with plenty of radio play. It didn't come as easy as some of her tracks, as she told the Radio 1 Podcast Interview 'We re-recorded that four times because we could not find the key that I could nail it in.'

She sings pretty high on *Good Luck, Babe*! 'I have songs that are higher, but the consonants that I'm saying are what make it difficult,' she said.

Although most of her songs are hard to sing and certainly not for the faint-hearted on a karaoke night.

It was released as a standalone track, and went to #1 in Ireland, #2 in the UK and #4 in the US, Canada and Australia. It was streamed over 106 million times on Spotify within months of its release.

The New York Times said the song was '...simply a great song, tightly written and hook-driven with a direct melody.'

Chappell has described it as 'the first chapter of the new book that I'm writing...I'm going to follow what I did for the last record, which is to write music that I love and put it out and with no other agenda than to have a great time on stage and make something that I'm proud of. As I write songs I love I'll put them out and eventually I will get a collection and release an album'.

Roan at the MTV Video Music Awards, New York, 2024

By **summer 2024** Chappell Roan was **impossible to miss.**

After her appearance on NPR's Tiny Desk concert series in March 2024, which went viral, Chappell followed up with standout live sets during the summer festival season.

Huge impact on Tiny Desk - March 2024

Chappell's vocally assured presentation of a stunning set of songs from *The Rise and Fall of a Midwest Princess* would have caused a stir, even if they had not been sung by her dressed in such a visually impactful way. Her huge red wig, adorned with butterfly clips and cigarette butts, topped off a full white face, made up with blue eyeshadow and red lips, with the lipstick also smeared across her teeth.

Chappell delivers a performance to remember on NPR's Tiny Desk, 2024

:: *Chappell Roan:* Icon of our times

Storming Coachella - April 2024

Performing on both weekends, April 12 and 19, Chappell's sets at Coachella truly transformed her career, going viral and setting social media aflame as she debuted her new song and queer anthem, *Good Luck, Babe!*

This is also where she famously coined the phrase, 'I'm your favourite artist's favourite artist', which was a reference to her drag 'mother' Sasha Colby who said 'I am your favourite drag queen's favourite drag queen' in her 2023 RuPaul's Drag Race 'Meet the Queens' cast reveal video.

'That hit me through the heart and that's why I said it,' said Chappell as she became an instant legend at the show.

NME described Chappell as having turned the Gobi tent into 'one big huddle of euphoria and joy. The rapturous response, coupled with her infectious, theatrical stage presence, conjured images of a steady climb through the festival's ranks for Roan to come, hopefully ending at the very summit of the bill.'

Coachella was a paradigm shift in Chappell's career. 'It's a zeitgeist moment and you can't manufacture it,' said booking agent Jackie Valpant in an interview.

Chappell takes Coachella by storm, California, 2024

Performing at the Governors Ball as the Statue of Liberty in New York City, 2024

Governors Ball - June 2024

Entering the New York stage from a giant apple, Chappell was dressed as 'the biggest queen of them all' – the Statue of Liberty – painted head to toe in green, brandishing a torch. "It was a complete transformation of the entire festival," said Huston Powell, a promoter at the company that booked the event. 'It felt like Chappell Roan mania. It felt like everybody wanted to see her.'

During her set she advocated for trans rights and announced that she had turned down an opportunity to perform at the White House during Pride month, because, 'We want liberty, justice, and freedom for all. When you do that, that's when I'll come.'

Going loopy at Lollapalooza - August 2024

Next came her set at Lollapalooza in Chicago, which was estimated to be the festival's largest crowd ever at 100,000 spectators, despite Chappell not being even among the headliners. As her manager Nick Bobetsky observed in an interview with Music Worldwide Business, ' The success hasn't taken her away from her core fans, she's taken them with her; they are part of it. That's why Lollapalooza was so impactful, because everybody was ready for it and everybody celebrated it, together with Roan. That's powerful – and infectious.'

Chappell brings the vocals and the latex to Lollapalooza at Grant Park, Chicago, 2024

Va va voom at the 2024 VMAs - September 2024

Chappell rounded off a truly astonishing year with a win as Best New Artist at the 2024 MTV Video Music Awards. She beat Teddy Swims, Gracie Abrams, Shaboozey and Tyla for the prize, dedicating her win to 'the queer and trans people who fuel pop' and a shout-out to 'queer kids in the Midwest watching right now.'

'I see you, I understand you because I am one of you,' she said. 'And don't ever let anyone tell you that you can't be exactly who you want to be.'

Her hit track *Good Luck, Babe!* was nominated at the same awards as '*Song of Summer*'.

Chappell was up against similarly tough competition, including towering artists Charli XCX, Billie Eilish, Ariana Grande, Sabrina Carpenter, and the eventual winner Taylor Swift with Fortnight, featuring Post Malone.

If the win and nomination weren't honour enough, Chappell was invited to perform – and boy did she make the most of the opportunity.

Chappell Roan poses with her Best New Artist award at the 2024 MTV Video Music Awards in New York, 2024

After an introduction by Chappell's drag mother and idol Sasha Colby, she arrived on stage wearing a full set of chainmail armour and carrying a crossbow, via the gates of a burning castle. Her jaw-dropping performance included a section where she fought off a chivalry of sword-carrying knights.

In between all those live shows came televised performances on The Late Show with Stephen Colbert, The Tonight Show Starring Jimmy Fallon, the 2024 Music Video Awards, and Saturday Night Live.

Chappell Roan performs on stage during the 2024 MTV Video Music Awards in New York, 2024

I try to be the chill girl

Chapter 9

I try to be the chill girl

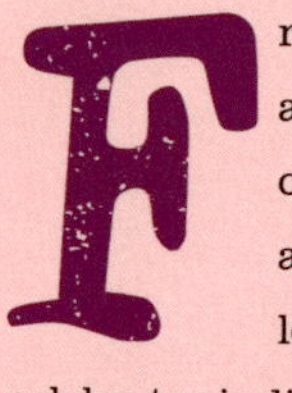

rom overcoming anxiety to fighting for her artistic freedom, each personal and professional challenge has shaped Chappell into a fierce advocate for authenticity in music. The enduring legacy she is carving in the music industry celebrates individuality, resilience, and the transformative power of music.

Chappell has been open about her issues with mental health and a bipolar diagnosis, challenges that have influenced her music and personal life. Her journey through these struggles has been a source of inspiration for many fans.

Speaking to Tom Power on the *Q* entertainment podcast, she said that if she could go back in time she would assure her 17-year-old self that 'she's a good person, she's enough and she's cool'. ' When you're bipolar and severely depressed there are so many lies that depression tells you. These feelings are temporary and you are a good person', she said.

'Chappell is a very exhausting character to play,' she continued. 'I try to protect myself. You have to prioritise yourself and your mental health. At the end of the day it's pop music, it's just a job and I don't plan on doing this forever so I need an identity outside of this so in 20 years from now I am not burnt out on life.'

As she said in a pre-fame article with *Cherwell* magazine, she finds social media to be the most demanding part of her 'job'. 'I can't really hate on it because it's pushed me forward and people know about me because of it, though it's the most soul-sucking part of my job. ... It's not hard. It's a 15-second video. But that's not the point. To some people, it comes naturally, and those people really soar, so it makes you feel bad about yourself if you try hard and it doesn't work.'

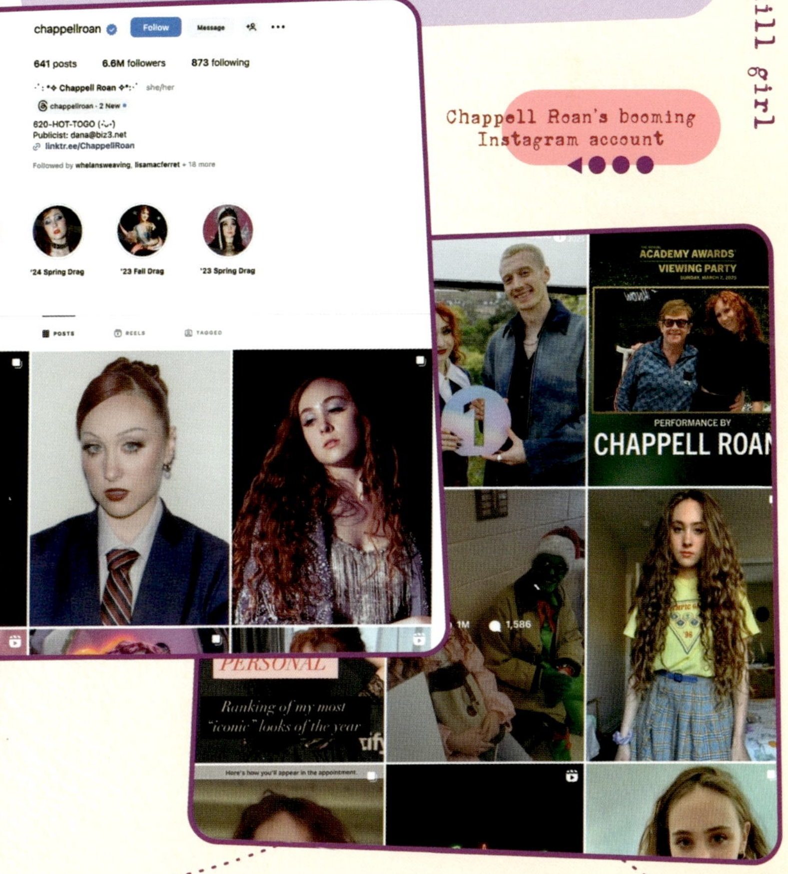

Chappell Roan's booming Instagram account

In a 2024 interview with the UK's *Guardian* newspaper, she spoke honestly about how her incredible rise to fame has affected her, saying that she has been diagnosed with 'severe depression' necessitating twice-weekly therapy and some psychiatric appointments.

She's not afraid of sharing her health with fans, and calling them out when she feels it's necessary.

At a show in June 2024, she announced on stage that she was finding it 'really hard to keep up,' and her tearful moment went viral.

She also put out a statement about invasive fan behaviour. 'I'm not in a delusion of, "Oh this is normal," she says of her current life. 'Like, this is very abnormal.'

There is a general understanding in the drag world that you do not approach a queen for a picture when she's out of costume. Chappell has signalled that 'Chappell' is a drag persona, and when out of costume and back to being 'Kayleigh', she has asked for similar privacy and respect.

Roan at the Spotlight Saturdays at the GRAMMY Museum L.A. Live, 2024

She has nevertheless been hassled and stalked by some fans. And in social media posts which offended some of her fandom she said that she 'doesn't give a f*ck' if she's described as 'selfish' for declining hugs and photos with strangers. 'That's not normal,' she says of those who demand a photo. 'That's weird. That's f***ing weird.'

'If you saw a random woman on the street, would you yell at her from the car window? Would you harass her in public?' I'm a random b**ch. You're a random b**ch. Just think about it.'

"All the News That Fits"
VOTE! VOTE! VOTE!
ELECTION 2
SPECIAL SECTION
A Star Is Born
CHAPPELL
ROAN
VOTE! VOTE! VOTE!

She has also joined the growing number of female celebrities who are speaking out about the negative treatment they receive.

In August 2024 she called out 'predatory behaviour (disguised as 'superfan' behaviour) that has become normalised because of the way women who are well-known have been treated in the past'. 'I don't care that abuse, harassment, stalking, whatever, is a normal thing to do to people who are famous... that does not make it okay,' she said.

Then in her cover story with Rolling Stone magazine, Chappell outlined some of the harassment she has faced including the arrival of a stalker at her parents' home and again at her hotel room, and a fan grabbing and then kissing her non-consensually while she was 'off duty' with friends in a bar.

Chappell is certainly not into developing the parasocial relationship with fans and has established strict ground rules for her off-stage interactions, including refusing to sign people's bodies so that they can have her signature tattooed. She also prefers that fans call her by her stage name.

"Everything that I really love to do now comes with baggage,' she told the UK's Guardian newspaper. 'If I want to go thrifting, I have to book security and prepare myself that this is not going to be normal," she said. "Going to the park, pilates, yoga – how do I do this in a safe way where I'm not going to be stalked or harassed?"

Chappell Roan features on the cover of *Rolling Stone* magazine, October 2024

Roan backstage serving retro glam

This inability to go about her previous everyday life happened so fast that she is still processing it.

In the *Guardian* interview she confided that "every time I walk through my front door" she starts to cry. 'It just comes out of me,' she said.

'I can't even help it, I just start sobbing and either being so angry at myself for choosing this path or grieving how the curiosity and pure wonder I had about the world is somewhat taken away from me.'

Though she believes she is experiencing fame as a process of grief, she is also intent on using her platform to make change. According to the *Guardian*, £1 of every one of her UK tour tickets went to LGBTQ+ charity Kaleidoscope Trust.

And despite the difficulties around fame, she also never forgets the important and privileged part she plays in representing the LGBTQ+ community. 'I know how hard it is to be queer in the Midwest and South' she says. 'I understand. And so I'm very grateful I can be here. And I just have to remind myself that this is why I do it... I hope you know that you are wanted here, and you're welcome here.'

She doesn't want fans to get the wrong idea. 'They think I'm complaining about my success,' she told the Guardian. 'I'm complaining about being abused.'

I'll take this city

Chapter 10

happell and Dan Nigro have been working on her second album since mid-2024 – and fans simply can't wait.

She has teased a few of the tracks, including country-style song *The Giver,* which she sang when she guested on Saturday Night Live in October 2024. It is a fun, up-tempo love song with an explicitly queer lyric including the sentiment that only a woman 'gets the job done' - a phrase which fans had seen on her Instagram and taken to be the song's title.

In an interview with *The New York Times,* Dan Nigro said, 'We have a country song. We have a dancy song. We have one that's really Eighties, and we have one that's acoustic, and we have one that's really organic, live-band, Seventies vibe. It's super weird'.

'It's a new version of Chappell,' Nigro said, including *The Subway*, a song she has been performing in concert, which is a more pensive number about seeing reminders of an old love.

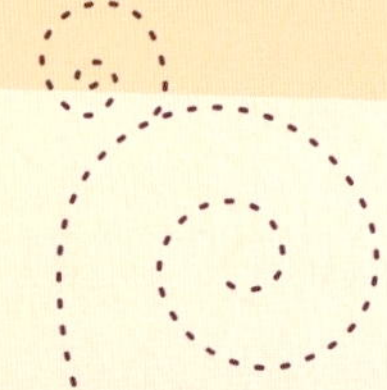

Crowds buzzing at the Austin City Limits Music Festival, Austin, Texas, 2024

From those glimpses it appears that Chappell will keep making robust, catchy anthemic pop songs, full of 'kiss-offs' and robust 'I've been through it' type tracks.

Her loyal fans will journey with her, despite her avowals never to compromise her private life to please them. As she told *Radio 1*, 'I never felt I was desperate for people to listen to me, have never been worried about gaining a fan base because it's something that you just can't force.'

Chappell word cloud

Queer, pop, trans rights, icon, Midwest princess, rhinestone, drag, explosive, innovative, bold, feminist, passion, drama, talent, playful, emotional, raunchy, proud, Gogo boots, pizzazz, provocative, camp, trashy, burlesque.

But she's forever grateful to her audience, which is always an integral part of her performance, joining in the singing and choreography which makes every concert a party.

Chappell's brave and declarative lyrics are helping to redefine what it means to be a modern pop star. By weaving her personal experiences with the universal conversation about what it means to be a modern woman, Chappell has become an important voice in the debate around empowerment. Not to mention elevating the expression of queerness in popular culture.

You can feel the roar around her as she rises up as the world's newest music star. She's a breath of fresh air in the pop ecosystem – representing something entirely different among female artists in the music industry.

Chappell Roan poster at Bonnaroo Music and Arts Festival in Manchester, TN, 2024

No one knows exactly what the future holds, but Chappell is sure to keep shifting and amplifying the status of queerness. She's honest and open and unlikely to waste the hard-fought celebrity status her fame now affords her.

Chappell's look at the Austin City Limits Music Festival, Texas, 2024

Chappell wins Best New Artist award at the 2025 GRAMMYs

She took her chance at the 2025 Grammy awards when she won the coveted Best New Artist award and used her acceptance speech to advocate for better support for artists from record companies.

'I told myself if I ever won a Grammy and I got to stand up here in front of the most powerful people in music, I would demand that labels and the industry profiting millions of dollars off of artists would offer a liveable wage and health care, especially to developing artists'.

'I got signed as a minor. And when I got dropped, I had zero job experience under my belt and like most people, I had a difficult time finding a job in the pandemic and could not afford health insurance'.

'Record labels need to treat their artists as valuable employees with a livable wage and health insurance and protection... Labels, we got you, but do you got us?'

While she maximises her new-found fame and works on new music, she is in a good place. She kicked off 2025 with her win as Best New Artist at the Grammy awards and five other Grammy nominations – including Best Pop Vocal Album, and Album of the Year for *The Rise and Fall of a Midwest Princess* and Best Pop Solo Performance, Song of the Year and Record of the Year for *Good Luck, Babe!*

As she told *Illustrate* magazine, 'I couldn't ask for more. It's not perfect but it's amazing.'

Discography

Album

The Rise and Fall of a Midwest Princess (2023)

EPs

Kayleigh Rose (2016)

School Nights (2017)

Singles

Die Young (2016)

Good Hurt (2017)

Sugar High (2017)

School Nights (2018)

Pink Pony Club (2020)

Love Me Anyway (2020)

California (2020)

Naked in Manhattan (2022)

My Kink is Karma (2022)

Femininomenon (2022)

Casual (2022)

Kaleidoscope (2023)

Red Wine Supernova (2023)

HOT TO GO! (2023)

Good Luck, Babe! (2024)

The Giver (scheduled for 2025)

Chappell Roan sets the stage ablaze performing *Pink Pony Club* at the 2025 GRAMMYs